War and Verse

Poetry & Prose of World War One
As seen in the Wartime Press
1914 - 1918

Edited by
Stephen Robert Kuta

Copyright

Re-invention U.K.

Published by Re-invention U.K.
Chelmsford
Essex
CM1 4JE

Printed by Lightning Source UK Ltd
Milton Keynes, Buckinghamshire, England

Copyright © 2018 Stephen Robert Kuta
www.stephenkuta.com

The moral rights of the author's have been asserted
Copyright © 2018 Re-invention U.K.

All Rights Reserved. No part of this publication may be reproduced, stored in a retrieval system, or transmitted, in any form or by any means, without prior permission in writing of Loma Publishing, or as expressly permitted by law, by licence or under terms agreed with the author.

Cover Image
Copyright © 2018 VEX Collective

A catalogue record for this book is available from the British Library.

First Edition
First Published 11th November 2018

ISBN: 978-0-9549899-2-7

Lest We Forget
In memory of the 10 million,
who died in action.
World War One (1914 - 1918)

World War One was one of the deadliest conflicts in the history of the human race, in which over 16 million people died. The total number of both civilian and military casualties is estimated at around 37 million people. The war killed almost 7 million civilians and 10 million military personnel.

Published Works

Anthologies

Paint the Sky with Stars
Editor / Published in 2005 in aid of raising money for the Tsunami Relief Fund /
Publisher: Re-invention U.K.

Once I Write of Love
Selected Poetry and Prose
Editor and Author / Published in 2018 / Publisher: Blurb Inc

War and Verse
Poetry & Prose of World War One
As seen in the Wartime Press
1914 - 1918
Editor / Published in 2018 / Publisher: Re-invention U.K.

Photography

1978 - 2018
My Life in Pictures
Published in 2018 / Publisher: Blurb Inc

History and Biography

The Lives of my Ancestors Series

Mrs Mary Plaskett (1739 - 1827)
Published in 2018 / Publisher: Blurb Inc

Selina's Letter
Tales of Suicide from Victorian and Edwardian London
Published in 2018 / Publisher: Loma Publishing

Contents

Page 11 - Forward

Page 19 - War and Verse
Page 23 - The light side of the war
Page 25 - In memory of an old friend
Page 27 - Freland in Flanders
Page 28 - Remembering's
Page 29 - His sacrifice
Page 30 - The failures
Page 31 - How the brothers met
Page 32 - At Charing Cross
Page 33 - The mother of dug-outs
Page 35 - Bill Smith's chum says
Page 38 - R.F.A.
Page 39 - The valley of the shadow
Page 40 - Letters
Page 41 - Two summer evenings
Page 42 - Disarmed
Page 43 - Missing
Page 44 - June in Picardy
Page 45 - A Fragment
Page 46 - Dawn
Page 47 - Rowans
Page 48 - Agincourt - and after
Page 50 - Pray for our dead

Page 51 - The great contrast
Page 52 - God's acre in France
Page 53 - An Indian's grave
Page 54 - The crimson cross
Page 55 - To a sister in France
Page 56 - Untitled
Page 58 - World war one nursery rhyme
Page 62 - The tryst
Page 63 - To old friends who fell at the Marne
Page 64 - The welcome
Page 65 - Two
Page 66 - The game
Page 67 - In memory of an airman
Page 68 - Untitled
Page 69 - Untitled
Page 70 - Oblivion
Page 71 - The spectre of Arras
Page 72 - The new recruits
Page 74 - Usquequo, Domine?
Page 77 - France's hymn of hate
Page 79 - Hymn of hate
Page 81 - The last trek
Page 83 - Lines addressed to the only other Captain left in the B.E.F.
Page 86 - Winchester
Page 87 - Untitled
Page 88 - Untitled
Page 89 - The road to victory
Page 91 - Epitaph

Page 92 - Per Mare, Per Terram
Page 93 - The soul of the land
Page 94 - Home-coming
Page 95 - Tanks
Page 96 - Young soldiers
Page 98 - Na Poo
Page 102 - Gott Mitt Uns!
Page 103 - Highland lament
Page 105 - To the chestnut militant
Page 107 - A city sunset
Page 108 - A world of war
Page 109 - Peace and war
Page 110 - If Herrick had been a hun
Page 112 - Ingredients for a Christmas war story
Page 113 - A war nightmare
Page 115 - Two London boys
Page 116 - Her renunciation
Page 117 - Made in Britain
Page 121 - Holy Willies prayer
Page 124 - The rubaiyat of William the warlord
Page 127 - To all mothers and fathers whose sons have been killed in the war
Page 128 - The memorial shrine, Westminster
Page 129 - Untitled
Page 131 - A local war poem
Page 133 - The day
Page 133 - The glassy eyes of the dead?
Page 135 - A soldier's war poem
Page 137 - A war poem
Page 138 - A war poem

Forward

Hope and fear, terror and triumph

War and Verse is an anthology of works written mostly by the ordinary man and woman during the war years 1914 – 1918, the individual poems were published in both the national and regional newspapers and showcased for the first time collectively in this book.

Before social media, email or smartphones - even before television - the effect of the written word was even more powerful than it is today. Poetry has long been used as a way of expressing our emotions, but perhaps at no time was emotive energy so intensely transferred onto the page than in the heat of battle during World War One.

Maybe it is because war can bring about so many emotions: from humiliation to pride; from trepidation to hope; and from love to hatred. How and to whom emotions were directed in World War One could not always be pigeon holed. A solider might have just as much hatred for his own generals or politicians as he did for the enemy. Love may be felt not only for a family left behind at home, but also for fellow soldiers, and the country itself.

While there are a huge range of emotions which are displayed within World War One poetry, there is an undeniably tragic element which is a natural consequence of nearly 10 million dead on both sides over the course of the War, and many more civilians who lost their lives.

So let us start with one of the more bleak, yet powerful examples of World War One poetry: 'In Flanders Fields, by John McRae'

In Flanders Fields
By John McCrae

In Flanders fields the poppies blow
Between the crosses, row on row,
That mark our place; and in the sky
The larks, still bravely singing, fly
Scarce heard amid the guns below.

We are the Dead. Short days ago
We lived, felt dawn, saw sunset glow,
Loved and were loved, and now we lie,
In Flanders fields.

Take up our quarrel with the foe:
To you from failing hands we throw
The torch; be yours to hold it high.
If ye break faith with us who die
We shall not sleep, though poppies grow
In Flanders fields.

McRae was a Canadian lieutenant colonel who was inspired to write the poem after conducting the burial service for artillery officer Alexis Helmer in his role as Company Doctor. The hum of bird song beneath the rumble of the guns, which McRae describes in the poem, offers a glimmer of hope amidst the cruel scene. However, McRae seems to be implying that the soldiers who fight on bear the responsibility of winning the war so that the dead may rest in their graves. The association he makes between commemorating the fallen soldiers and the fields of poppies was said to have strengthened the connection which has now become popularised by Remembrance Sunday.

Next let's look at a poem which weaves melancholy with its words: 'Perhaps' by Vera Brittain.

The tragedy at the heart of this poem, penned in 1916, is the death of the poet's fiancé Roland Aubrey Leighton (1895-1915), who was killed by a sniper aged 20. Brittain had accepted Leighton's proposal for marriage only four months before he died. The consistent repetition of the word 'perhaps' throughout the poem gives it a form of uncertainty, but there also seems to be a sad resignation at the heart of the words. The poet appears to have been very depressed with the cards which life had dealt her, and is doubtful whether she will ever recover fully: "Perhaps some day I shall not shrink in pain." 'Perhaps' is a great example of a World War One poem which deals with the loss of a loved one, and its impact.

The sheer fragility of human life during World War One is almost hard to comprehend, but one of the best jobs in this regard is done by 'Break of Day in the Trenches' by Issac Rosenburg.

What seems like it could be an uplifting poem from the title is actually brutally frank about the chances of human survival in this dangerous theatre of trench warfare. In the verses, the poet describes encountering a rat, and then draws comparison between his own chances of survival and that of the rat - "Less chanced than you for life, Bonds to the whims of murder, Sprawled in the bowels of the earth." He seems almost to envy the rat's freedom to pass between the Allied and German trenches, and suggests that the creature can sense its own freedom in comparison to the soldiers' situation in the trench: "It seems you inwardly grin as you pass."

World War One demonstrated examples of solidarity between soldiers on both sides, as they fought a war which at times was reduced to a bloody stalemate. This was famously exemplified on Christmas Day, 1914, when hostilities ceased temporarily, and troops went out into 'No Man's Land' for a game of football. This sense of sharing the same fate is highlighted by 'To Germany', by Charles Hamilton Sorley.

An adept writer even at the age of 20, Charles Hamilton Sorley had the experience of studying in Germany prior to enrolling at Oxford University. Perhaps this contributed to the empathy which he demonstrated for the enemy in 'To Germany'. The line "you are blind like us" hints at anti-war sentiment, and that the soldiers on both sides were merely pawns in a game played by the higher powers. It also references the nature of Germany's imperial ambitions with the line "your future bigly planned". He wraps up the poem with a parting shot at the futility of the war, writing: "And in each other's dearest ways we stand, And hiss and hate. And the blind fight the blind."

Finally, let's look at a poem which brings out the sheer horror of experiences on the battlefield - 'Dulce et Decorum Est', by Wilfred Owen.

Dulce et Decorum Est
By Wilfred Owen

Bent double, like old beggars under sacks,
Knock-kneed, coughing like hags, we cursed through sludge,
Till on the haunting flares we turned our backs,
And towards our distant rest began to trudge.
Men marched asleep. Many had lost their boots,
But limped on, blood-shod. All went lame; all blind;
Drunk with fatigue; deaf even to the hoots
Of gas-shells dropping softly behind.

Gas! GAS! Quick, boys!—An ecstasy of fumbling
Fitting the clumsy helmets just in time,
But someone still was yelling out and stumbling
And flound'ring like a man in fire or lime.—
Dim through the misty panes and thick green light,
As under a green sea, I saw him drowning.

In all my dreams before my helpless sight,
He plunges at me, guttering, choking, drowning.

If in some smothering dreams, you too could pace
Behind the wagon that we flung him in,
And watch the white eyes writhing in his face,
His hanging face, like a devil's sick of sin;
If you could hear, at every jolt, the blood
Come gargling from the froth-corrupted lungs,
Obscene as cancer, bitter as the cud
Of vile, incurable sores on innocent tongues,—
My friend, you would not tell with such high zest

> To children ardent for some desperate glory,
> The old Lie: *Dulce et decorum est*
> *Pro patria mori.*

Wilred Owen wrote 'Dulce et Decorum Est' while recovering in a Scottish hospital after fighting in Northern France. The title refers to the latin ode of Horace, the Roman poet, and translates to "is sweet and proper to die for one's country". Describing the terror of a gas attack, Owen leaves the reader under no illusions that Dulce et Decorum Est does not ring true for this war. With his descriptions of panic in the wake of the attack "an ecstasy of fumbling", staring death in the face "he plunges at me, guttering, choking, drowning", and finally conveying the intensely disturbing experience "obscene as cancer, bitter as the cud", Owen delivers a graphic and haunting account of what it was like to fight in World War One.

Rhetoric of honour/soldier-poets

World War One poetry represents a broad range of different viewpoints and perspectives, but one common theme is the rhetoric of honour which is contrasted with descriptions of broken and injured bodies. This ability to describe the physical discomfort experienced on so many levels in the trenches - in the eyes, the mouth and the head - is often contextualised using the wider political narrative as a backdrop.

While some of the early poems of World War One favoured the first person, commonly referring to 'I', later poems - with 'To Germany', by Charles Hamilton Sorley being seen as a precursor - came to use 'You' more often, talking directly to the reader when describing the terrible scenes.

Why has First World War Poetry stood the test of time?

World War One poetry offers us history, culture, and powerful personal experiences. Because the written word offered the people who were affected by the War one of the only ways of chronicling their experiences, thoughts and feelings, it comes in many forms and offers numerous perspectives.

While World War One poetry might be seen as very 'English' in its nature, the number of other Anglo countries involved in the War - from Scotland to New Zealand and Canada - means that we are left with a truly international collection of poetry. Poetry from the War still works in the classroom, and perhaps there is no better way of teaching children about trench warfare than with poetry filled with vivid descriptions of the gas masks, barbed wire, mud and misery.

If you value poetry for its ability to transfer human emotion and carry human experience, World War One poetry has it all.

Stephen Robert Kuta

War and Verse
Poetry & Prose of World War One
As seen in the Wartime Press
1914 - 1918

The Light Side of the War:
As it is, as it isn't
A Quiet Day at Corps Headquarters

Observe a simple rustic scene,
The Corps Headquarters' croquet green,
Stretching in beauty far below
The windows of the old château:
And here, worn out by ceaseless work—
Which not a man would deign to shirk—
The General and his friends are playing.
The Staff, for once, is holidaying.
Most days, when all the work is done,
It's much too late for outdoor fun,
And there is nothing else to do
But play at ping-pong, whist or loo,
Or, if the General's in form,
Some blind man's buff to keep one warm.
To-day, however, all is glee,
The birthday of a D.A.G.
Has banished toil, and all are free
To snatch one afternoon of leisure,
And 'Neath the trees to roam at pleasure.
The General and a G.S.O.
School playmates in the long ago
Swollen with lunch and draughts of Tokay,
Engage in mimic strife at croquet.

But who is this, whose craggy face
Bears discipline's exacting trace
This stalwart figure on the right,
Symbolic of the Army's might Listen
The very tree trunks stir
"Drill Sergeant Blennerhasset, sir!
Bearer of very grave despatches…"

The A.D.C.s crowd round in batches,
And seek to drown the ill-omened voice
(They know bad news their Chief annoys).
Hush My good man," says Number 1,
This is a monstrous thing you've done,
To burst in here unintroduced.
I think you ought to be reduced
Go off and give your message to
The Q.A.G. or G.A.Q.,
But silence, please be quiet, I beg!
The G.S.O. has struck the peg,
And, "Whispering he scarcely spoke,
You'll put the General off his stroke."

Written by: Unknown
Published: Saturday 16th June 1917
Publication: The Graphic

In Memory of an Old Friend
Lieut.-Colonel Malcolm McNeil, C.M.G., D.S.O.,
Argyll and Sutherland Highlanders.
Soldier, Piper and Shikari.

I may not read the rune beyond the grave—
No traveller e'er returns from Death's long leave;
I know not of the bourne the soul must brave,
Or if for change or endless sleep I grieve.

But if your spirit brave be lodged again
In your brave body, so perfected new,
I Then I can see you striding through the rain
In some celestial Highlands of the blue.

I see you treading firm the piper's stride,
And hear the pibroch thrilling through the glen,
While dead Argylls, e'er earthly tears have dried,
I Shake off their shrouds to quit themselves as men.

While fingers twitch to grasp the phantom dirk,
And know again the claymore's hungry steel,
While Lome's great dead march proudly through the mirk,
To follow once again a proud McNeil.

Or chance I hear the pipes a-skirling fast,
See dirk or claymore swiftly cast away:
While saints and prophets stand in rows aghast,
As tartans whirl around the wild Strathspey.

I see by beetled scaur and fretted strath
Your stalker's eye discern the envied stag,
Or with your pet Somali seek the path
That swells the noble trophies of your bag.

And if your loyal senses still can reach
To Western islands sown amid the seas,
I swear you hear the drone upon the beach
Of running tides that wash the Hebrides.

If speech be yours, I ken the loyal tongue
I hat dwells with longing on the ancient thirst
Which drained the bowl of manhood oft among
Your hero comrades of the Ninety-First.

These be but fancies, creatures of the dreams
I weave to take the sting of death away.
How strange, McNeil! but. yesterday it seems
We ran amok in dreams at Colonsay!

Archibald Stodart Walker (1869 – 1934)

Published: Saturday 30 June 1917
Newspaper: The Graphic

Freland in Flanders

Deep in the trenches, patient, still,
Before Messines the Irish lay,
Whilst flame and thunder from the hill
Swept down on them by night and day.

Over the parapet like a flood,
Orange and green together go:
The lust of battle in their blood,
They burst upon the astonished foe.

Have at them, gallowglass and kern,
Whose fathers smote the Danish hosts!
Have at them, sinewy sons of Erne,
And men from storied Antrim's coasts!

High up the Orange Flag is seen
To crown the hard-contested height,
Beside it the immortal Green,
That never fell behind in fight.

Orange and Green charged side by side,
Resistless as a tidal wave:
For freedom fought, for freedom died,
And sleep within a common grave.

There discord may for ever cease:
For not in vain their blood was shed,
If North and South shake hands in peace
Above their consecrated dead.

J. Cuthbert Scott.
Published: Saturday 15th December 1917
Newspaper: The Graphic

Remembering's

The roses brim their crimson tides,
Their Junes in pink and white;
And mark their seal across their land,
Their land as hushed as night;
And if they miss a farther touch
Than sun from sunset throws,
Perhaps they do not care to tell
What just a rose-bud knows.

The thistles grow aloof and tall,
And purple with the heath;
And if their memoried days be long,
They reach to roots beneath.
Perhaps a thistle is all mute
To dearest things it sows;
Perhaps it holds the evening's stain,
Because a thistle knows.

The lilies cluster in a land
Of dreams, hued gold and white;
And they have written in her heart
The altar things of light;
The priceless things of years and love
That all the past bestows.
Perhaps the lilies told their bells,
Because a lily knows.

Virginia Stait.

Published: Saturday 19th October 1918
Newspaper: The Graphic

His Sacrifice
(On seeing a young nerve-wrecked soldier)

Condemned, ere boyhood's bloom had fled
The rounded cheek, to know through life
The quiv'ring nerves, the aching head,
The heart that failed in the strife;

To dream of deeds he could not bear,
And in the hours of darkest night
To see the dangers comrades share,
Hear echoes of the hell-born fight.

His life he gave not, but he gave
His peace of mind, his happy youth;
Not his the calm within the grave,
But living pain that knows no ruth.

He gave his country all that made
Life worthy of his love. And we
Do deem him for the price he paid
One of our heroes' company.

Elizabeth H. Shillito.

Published: Saturday 28th October 1916
Newspaper: The Graphic

The Failures
(On visiting the Graveyard of a School of Flying)

In many a grassy grave
They sleep, with none to tell
The tale of all they gave,
Who failed and fell

No honours from their King
E'er shone tip on their breast,
Swift plights on glitt'ring wing
And then-their rest.

Glad sons of air and sky,
Young conquerors of fear,
In triumph rode on high
And now-sleep here

'Neath quiet trees; yet still
These souls of flame and fire,
Unconquerable will,
Untold desire,

On higher wings shall rise
Above earth's ways, dust-trod,
Children of Morning Skies,
Fair sons of God.

Elizabeth H. Shillito.

Published: Saturday 5th October 1918
Newspaper: The Graphic

How the Brothers Met

They quarrelled, parted with a frown.
Took each his several path;
And that, and many a day went down
And rose upon their wrath.

And Jim went east and Duncan west;
And not a word said Jim,
And Duncan well, he would be blest
Before he'd speak to him.

The tranquil hamlet of their birth
The brothers left behind;
Wider between them grew the earth.
And keener blew the wind.

In 'Frisco, where the cypress waves
Its melancholy green.
Are James and Duncan Gordon's graves
And not a step between.

James Logie Robertson (1846 – 1922)

Published: Saturday 12th March 1921
Newspaper: The Graphic

At Charing Cross

By day and night the tides sweep out and in;
Now, on the ebb our boys are carried far;
To deeps in which the new life will begin,
Where storm and death and hell and glory are.

Now, on the inward tide grave mercy bears
Some home for ever, some a little space,
Boys, who in days have lived through many years-
Wise to see Life through Death's familiar face.

Edward Shillito. (1872 – 1948)

Published Saturday 5th August 1916
Newspaper: The Graphic

The Mother of Dug-outs

I'VE come from a "dug-out" in Flanders,
From the mud, the blood, and the doubt;
I've come to a city that panders
To the men who haven't been out.

When the date of my leave was certain
I thought, as I hurled hand-grenades,
Of the ladies "behind the curtain"
And the fun of the Promenades.

I thought of the music and laughter,
The Song, the Passion, the Dance;
I thought of the bad head-aches after,
And the wearisome journey through France.

But I've come to a city of doom:
No Song, no Women, no Wine,
And I wander about in the gloom,
Searching for somewhere to dine.

The rest'rants are full of the others:
Of traders, shirkers and spies,
Home-service men and their mothers,
And the men who are held by home ties.

The night-clubs are closed at twelve- thirty,
The bright promenades are all bare.
In the streets that are darkened and dirty,
That's where you'll find them-there.

Are we a nation defeated-
To be spat upon, jeered at and cursed—
Or are all these changes completed
By the plan that a Great Prig has nursed?

I want to go back to excitement,
To laughter, whiskey, and shell,
To life's joy and pain death's enlightenment-
I want to go back to Hell.

Ronald Frankau (1894 – 1951)
Published: Wednesday 16th February 1916
Newspaper: The Bystander

Bill Smith's Chum says

What d'ye think we're doin',
Mam and the girls and me,
Sittin' down in the drill-hall,
All busy as busy can be?
And the old chap round the comer,
And the boy that wants a leg,
And the big, brown gent from India,
What talks 0' havin' a peg,"
And the ladies up from the grand hotel,
All covered wi' diamond rings,
And the little white-faced orphan
That stands in the street and sings;
Now, what d'ye think we're doin'?-
Prayer-meetin' Pitch and toss?
A h, well, ye'd better give it up, for ye' d never guess
Why, we're all of us pickin' moss!

Moss from the silent moorland,
Moss from the green braeside-
And it's goin' away in the troopships
That sail wi' the windy tide;
It's goin' to France and Belgium,
To the Ancre and the Somme-
Some of it's goin' to Egypt,
Maybe some of it's bidin' at home;
But all of it's goin' to someone-
(My Don't the thing sound queer?)
To someone who's sheddin' his blood for us
All sittin' so cosy here.
Our moss wi' the sun upon it,
And Highland rain and dew,
Growin' in God's own garden,
Dear soldier lads, for you.

Pickin' moss for the soldiers!
It's the finest ploy we have
It's jest all Hist' ry pipin' hot,
'Bout Teuton, Gaul and Slav-
It's the war loohin' in at the window,
And the whizz-bangs goin' by,
And our khakis standin' row on row,
'Neath the blue of a far-off sky.
Or maybe 't's the dusk that's fallin'
Wi' our khakis lyin' still,
Face down in the clay as they told us
On the crest of Hulluch Hill.
...Well, that's where the moss is goin',
And you'd like it if you knew
What dear queer things go with it,
Oh, soldier lads, to you.

There's Betty, look, in the corner.
She sits and wipes her eyes,
And once we would ha' laughed at her
Wi' her snuffly sobs and sighs;
But we don't laugh now worth mentionin'
My chum, Bill Smith, an' me,
'Cause we think of the boy as she lost last year Away in the cold North Sea.
...Oh, yes, it's the moss we're doin'
But, by gum the moss ain't all;
There's a mighty lot 0' thinkin'
Been done in this 'ere hall.
Why, folks as were hardly speakin'
An', hatin' each other like mad,
Jest over the moss has been lovin an' kind
As they think 0' some soldier lad
Who's fightin' away out yonder,
Fightin' for Earth's Big Things,
An' makin' them sick ashamed o' sulks
An' swappin' digs an' flings.
... Ay, I think we're growin' better,
Kinder and straighter too,
An' its all along 0' the moss, you -know,
An', soldier lads, o' you,

Mary Symon

Published: Saturday 12th May 1917
Newspaper: The Graphic

R.F.A.
A Tribute to the Battery Chestnut who fell for England.

The chestnut never had a name
For she was no one's special nag,
But did her bit when autumn came
A -hunting of the drag.

Some pulled her mouth until it bled,
Some rowelled her and made her prance,
And England, being sore bestead,
Then shipped her into France,

Where, through the dazing cannonade,
She and her comrades were in stress.
She could not sleep, nor eat (poor jade!)
Sometimes (for weariness)

Her frugal feed. The man was slain
Who was her driver; where he fell
Another caught the dangling rein
And rode her into hell.

He rode her (so a swimmer rides
A wave) "quo fas et Gloria
Ducunt" the team, with heaving sides,
Right gamely followed they

And saved the gun. She paid her toll;
Where pyres are lit for sepulchre
Her body lies, but not her soul-
Valhalla pastures her.

C.M.J

Published: Saturday 27th January 1917
Newspaper: The Graphic

The Valley of the Shadow

"All still on the line." So official reporter
Will send to the Press the report of last night.
'Tis true! No battalions leapt out to the slaughter
'Neath the bursting of shells or the scream of their flight.

Crouched in my dug out, I passed the long hours,
And watched the pale moon to the parapet sink.
Rats- fearful no longer of man or his powers-
Made fetid the air with their carrion stink.

"All still on the line!" Past the square, sand bag setting
That stood for a door in the shadowy gloom
Two figures passed upright, the night silhouetting
A third, very still, 'gainst the sheen of the moon.

Just a stray shot from a casual sniper
Guided by Death across No Man's Land,
And His human harvest to-night is riper
As the pick falls down from the sapper's hand.

"Only one man"-'tis the hourly story,
Too trivial, far, for the bulletin board!
No florid columns shall pean his glory.
"All still on the line" is their only word.

Yet somewhere beyond the white cliffs of Dover
Two hearts-a young and an old-shall break;
The old for a son, the young for a lover,
That is dead for theirs and for England's sake.

Written by: J. H. O'Kelly
Published: Saturday 27th January 1917
Newspaper: The Graphic

Letters

A little packet, ribbon-tied
The letters that we had from him,
We read them over, misty-eyed,
Eyes that are yet with tear-drops dim.
Brief, simple letters, all unschool'd,
Just such as any boy might send,
On writing-pad all neatly ruled,
To father, mother, sister, friend.

Remembrances to friends at home,
'The rumours of the great advance,
A parcel, letter, safely come,
Censored each one "somewhere in France."
We smile even thro' our tears, for, oh,
The enemy might safely read
"I'm thinking of you all, you know,
Here in this dug-out with a weed."

Those letters ceased at last to come.
Dear God, they will not come again!
And that last brief one from the Somme,
We read it o'er and o'er with pain.
Yet is it well, O soldier dear,
In some far clime by us untrod,
Thou'rt still, with heart that knows not fear,
"On active service"- for thy God.

Written by: Frank Ellis.
Published: Saturday 28th July 1917
Newspaper: The Graphic

Two Summer Evenings

1900

A summer's eve, and it's nearly dark,
A young mother watches her boy.
She smiles on the sleeping babe, and, hark!
How the birds sing after day's joy!
"Go to sleep! He's asleep!-
And she looks. They sing true:
He's asleep yes, asleep!

1918.

A summer's eve, and it's nearly dark.
The Mother stands in his room.
The boy has been killed in France; but, hark!
How the birds sing out in the gloom!
"He's asleep-yes, asleep"-
And she knows. They sing true:
He's asleep-yes, asleep!

Written By J.A.C., a Poet of Fourteen
Published: Saturday 27th July 1918
Newspaper: The Graphic

Disarmed

When Night comes down, unnumbered ghosts
   Stalk through the gloom of sea and plain
   To where Hell gapes, and warring hosts
   Bring death and horror in their train.

The patient trees, all maimed and marred,
   Appeal to Heaven for peace and rest;
Earth wounded, bleeding, battle-scarred,
   Gathers her dead sons to her breast.

Grim Winter, borne on piercing gales,
   With spear of ice upraised to smile,
   Sudden relents and softly veils
Sad earth in robes of stainless white.

Written by: J. Cuthbert Scott.
Published: Saturday 26th January 1918
Newspaper: The Graphic

Missing

Some own a bit of daisied turf at home,
For some, six feet of earth in France may hold him fast;
Some, looking hard into a world beyond,
Find him at last.

But I have no such certain hope and sure.
To me no Voice cries from the sky or ground,
Neither in earth or Heaven, by sea or shore,
May he be found.

'Tis ill for them that lose their mates outright,
Though some still greet him when his children call;
But she who's neither widow,
mother, maid nor wife,
She has lost all.

Written by: E. M. Wilmot Buxton.
Published: Saturday 26th January 1918
Newspaper: The Graphic

June in Picardy

There are roses on the cottage fronts in France, lass,
Roses pink and yellow, crimson-red and white.
When I pass them, oh how wistfully I glance, lass,
How my sad thoughts dwell on days of past delight!

Do the roses on our cottage front at Home, lass,
Tap your window in the morning? do they gleam,
Fragrant phantoms, in the twilight, while I roam, lass,
These foreign fields, and ache for you and them?

Will there come again a June for you and me, lass,
When together in the quiet night we lean
From your window, where the roses climb, and see, lass,
In each other's eyes what life and heaven mean

Written by: Hamilton Fyfe (1869 – 1951)
Published: Saturday 15th June 1918
Newspaper: The Graphic

A Fragment

Beloved England-faint of heart they said,
Drugged with the glory of resplendent days,
Wearing thy laurels withered on thy head,
As beauty passing to autumnal days.

They wronged thee-England-'twas thy triumph hour,
To show thou keptst the faith in freedom's power,
And thou hast answered, great and royally,
In myriads of thy dead in foreign fields.

Thy robes of glory ne'er will faded be,
While thy sons pour their blood in crimson tide.
Thou wilt remain for ages great and free,
If honour be thy path and God thy guide.

Written by: William O. Jones.
Published: Saturday 15th June 1918
Newspaper: The Graphic

Dawn

Dawn paints her thousand colours on the sky,
Purple with pride, pale with despair,
Dark with dissimulation, all are there.

These lights and shadows follow us through life,
Illuminating all our path,
Then screening the dread aftermath;

A pause or two-light and then shade-
The shadows deepen,
And the trail is made.

Written by: Kathleen Conway.
Published: Saturday 20th January 1917
Newspaper: The Graphic

Rowans

When in the glen he stood with me,
　　My heart's desire,
The rowans on the trysting tree
　　Were drops of fire.

But now he lies in France, and dead
　　Are leaf and bud;
The rowans on the tree are red
　　With his heart's blood.

Written by: J. Cuthbert Scott
Published: Saturday 20th January 1917
Newspaper: The Graphic

Agincourt – and After
1415 – October 25 – 1915
The 500th Anniversary of St. Crispin's Day

Khaki for corselet, guns for bows,
Shrapnel and gas for the grey goose wing,
Savage instead of chivalrous foes;
All has been changed since Harry the king
Five hundred years ago to-day
Won against odds that famous fray.

Once more upon the vasty fields of France
The yeomen of old England face the foe,
Once more unto the breach they now advance
As did their forebears all those years ago.

Once more the youth of England are on fire
And strain upon the start, with hearts aglow,
To prove that each is worthy of his sire
Who fought in France five hundred years ago.

Once more with noble lustre in their eyes
Our men the mettle of their pasture show,
Once more the precious English blood bedyes
The soil of half a thousand years ago.

Once more those cull' d and choice-drawn cavaliers.
Whose limbs were made in England, let us know
Our little isle, despite unworthy fears,
Grows heroes of the breed of long ago.

Khaki for corselet, guns for bows,
Fire-spray and bomb for the grey goose wing,
Germans instead of French for foes;
All has been changed save one single thing:
The soul of England flames as pure
As on the day of Agincourt.

Written by: W. K. C.
Published: Saturday 23rd October 1915
Newspaper: The Graphic

Pray for Our Dead

All ye who kneel at home beside a bed, Redeemed and safe because of countless dead, Pray for Those Dead.

Pray for Our Dead: They may not' need our prayers-
Indeed I think we have more need of theirs:
Yet lift your souls for Them to One Who Knows
The Curtained Door through which the spirit goes:
PRAY FOR THE DEAD.

It well may be prayers fall upon their road,
And blossom it, up all Their way to God;
Or it may be that at Their journeys' ends
Our prayers shall find Them Messages from friends-
PRAY FOR OUR DEAD

Perchance by prayers we touch Their garments' hem,
And thus receive new virtue out from Them:
Howe'er it be, of this I am assured
Tis well to pray for Spirits which endured-
PRAY FOR THE DEAD.

All ye who kneel at home beside a bed, Redeemed and safe because of countless dead, Pray for Those Dead.

Written by: Jessie Annie Anderson.
Published: Saturday 27th April 1918
Newspaper: The Graphic

The Great Contrast

This is the day of France,
The land of high romance,
With Freedom's flag unfurled
Once more she leads the world.
She never hymned "The Day,'
Our gallant Gaul, And yet her Day has come;
We never heard her say
"France over all!"
To sound of fife and drum;
Until she could obey
The trumpet-call
The voice of France was dumb.
The long suspense is past,
'Tis France's Day at last.
Advance, and break a lance
For Freedom and for France

Written by: W. K. C.
Published: Saturday 17th July 1915
Newspaper: The Graphic

God's Acre in France

In the sweet bosom of this hill,
Where the load noise of gun is still,
Where clash of armies is unheard,
And all is still save note of bird.
Gathered into their early grave,
Here sleep the young, the proud, the brave.

The veteran of a score of fights,
Who oft has tasted war's delights,
Tis meet that he should fight once more,
And add a scar to those he bore.
But these so young, so fair, so dear,
These English boys, what do they here?

They look their place within the line,
They knew no fear, they gave no sign.
They stood amid the battle cries
With the young laughter in their eyes.
Wounded they winced not, pain defied,
And when their hour came, smiling died.

When the last booming gun is still
Fond hearts shall visit this sweet hill,
Pause by this consecrated sod,
This sacred A ere owned of God,
And drop, where these young lives have died,
One only tear-and that of Pride.

Written by: Frank Ellis.
Published: Saturday 14th July 1917
Newspaper: The Graphic

An Indian's Grave
(In France)

The Way-there is but one for East and West,
Our choosing or forsaking-
That lies through good to ill, through toil to rest,
Through rest to waking.

He came in loving faith, with eyes that sought
Through life's tumultuous blinding;
And that great moment dawned wherein was wrought
Rapture of finding.

And now, a simple token at his grave,
Half-seeing, all-believing,
He starts a further pilgrimage of brave
And loyal achieving.

Written by: Arthur L. Salmon.
Published: Saturday 19th August 1916
Newspaper: The Graphic

The Crimson Cross

Across the shell-torn plains of France,
Amid the havoc, blood and pain,
There shines a steady, flaming light
That cleaves the darkness like a lance,
And brings good- cheer and strength again
To those who faint beneath the night.

The glowing ray, far-reaching, strong,
Comes blazing from a Crimson Cross,
That calmly dares War's hideous woe
To aid in righting deadly wrong,
To comfort those made mad by loss
And succour broken friend and foe.

Dyed red with blood of countless wars
It steadfast shines a fiery sign
Of mercy, soltice, love all three;
And men who march thro' Hell's wide doors,
In passing, murmur down the line
"We, about to die, salute thee!"

Written by: Hellen Margaret Richmond.
Published: Saturday 17th August 1918
Newspaper: The Graphic

To a Sister in France (Lines written on being invalided home)

While our strength was but small,
And we lingered abed,
How you cared for us all-
We were kiddies, you said;
Some of us five, and some only two.
It was good to be mothered by you!

When we tossed through the night,
Till we drowsed, you would stay;
And then, "Shut your eyes tight,"
With a smile you would say.
"Shut your eyes tight, and go to sleep, do!"
It was great to be mothered by you!

Yes, you smiled through the gloam,
And my battle was won;
And a mother at home
Gives you thanks for her son,
Joining with many a woman too
Whose big "boy" has been mothered by you.

Written by: Fred W. Bayliss, / Published: Saturday 17th August 1918 /
Newspaper: The Graphic
INTIMATES From a Hospital in France.

Untitled

We played at comrades, you and I;
Chance made me pawn and you the queen,
And we debated earnestly
How things that were not might have been.

We marched adown the gold-paved way;
We held our state in royal halls,
As though the earth's empiric sway
Were bounded by these naked walls.

Till ever in your wise concern
My weakness served your kinder will,
That watched the fevered taper burn,
And slaved to keep it burning still.

You smiled by lamplight at the trace
Of child surrender on the deep
Serenity of my wan face,
The immortality of sleep.

And once we hearkened to the rain
Throughout the long companioned night
Till dawn crept to the window-pane
And touched the walls with timid light.

'Tis strange the lot that haunts me still;
That I should fail my part despite
The power to guide the flesh by will;
That you should stand my watch by night.

Even hours of forfeit shall reward
Who, by their chance, must watch and wait;
So first within this prisoned ward
I touched your hand upon the gate.

If we hereafter may not meet,
You will be strong nor grieve too much,
Knowing each faithful hand I greet
Stirs with the spirit of your touch.

Just as in petals of faded flowers,
A beauty haunts there without end;
As perfuire through the wasting hours,
The memory lingers of a friend.

In other land, perhaps you'll tell
some dearer friend, whose faith you try,
"There's fragrance in old flowers" ah, well,
We played at comrades, you and I

Written by: Danford Barney
Published: Saturday 16th November 1918
Newspaper: The Graphic

World War One Nursery Rhyme
Published: Wednesday 14th February 1917
Newspaper: The Bystander

#1 - Little Colquhoun

Little Colquhoun has lost his Platoon,
And doesn't know where to find them.
I Leave them alone and they'll come home-
When estaminets close behind them.

#2 - Clumsy Rumsey

Clumsy Rumsey sat on a bomb
(Prim'd and percussed) with pointless aplomb,
All the King's nurses and medical men
Couldn't have put them together again.

#3 - Sing a Song of "Strafling"

Sing a song of "Strafling" a trench full of mud,
Four-and-twenty- "minnies", and not a single dud!
When the ball was opened by our blessed guns,
Wasn't it a stupid thing to irritate the Huns?

#4 - "Beer", "Beer" Battery

" 'Beer', 'Beer', Battery, have you any shells?"
"Yes, Sir, yes-what America sells.
Some for the Boche, and some for the 'blue,'
And some for our own front parapet, too."

#5 - Trickle, Trickle, Little Jar

Trickle, trickle, little jar,
What a wondrous thing you are!
My moral is always high,
When the morning rum is nigh.

#6 – Private Jack Horner (1st Version)

Private Jack Horner
Sat in a corner
Holding a Mills Grenade.
I relate with chagrin
That he pulled out the pin-
What an awful mistake he made!

#7 – Private Jack Horner (2nd Version)
Private Jack Horner
Found in a corner
Boxes-one, registered "Rum"
He said-yes, he did,
When he pulled off the lid,
And found it was "apple and plum".

#8 – Hausfrau Von Hurst

Hausfrau Von Hurst
Went to buy wurst
To put on her family's plates.
When she got there
The butchers was bare,
And so the poor family "hates".

#9 – Lieutenant Muffet

Lieutenant Muffet
Sat in a "buffet"
Absorbing aperitifs many.
A demoiselle spied him,
And sat down beside him;
But that didn't frighten him any.

#10 – Sapper Boy True

"Sapper boy true, come, blow up your mine;
There are hundreds of Huns in the opposite line.
Oh! Where is the man who looks after the fuse?"
"He's down in the dug-out, Sir, having a snooze".

#11 – Simple Sapper

Simple Sapper met a flapper
On the boulevard.
Suggested Sapper to the flapper
"Compris Promenade?"
Cautious flapper questioned Sapper,
"Ave you leetle money?"
Saddened Sapper sighed to flapper,
"Napoo, je suis 'stony."

#12 – Party, Party, Working Party

"Party, party, working party,
How does the wiring go,
With pickets, screw, and wire,
Barbed, new, and knife-rests all in a row?"
"Oh, damn the pickets, and damn the wire, and damn the knife-rests too!"
(Which isn't exactly nursery talk, but it's just what soldiers do.)

#13 - Ten Private Soldiers going up the line

Ten Private Soldiers going up the line,
One had trouble with a "five-point-nine."
Nine Private Soldiers, hiding from the "hate,"
One thought it cowardly and then there were eight.
Eight Private Soldiers, sandbagging to Heaven,
Spotted by the Hun and then there were seven.
Seven Private Soldiers, pottering with picks,
One struck something and then there were six.
Six Private Soldiers tried to keep alive,
One was a failure and then there were five.
Five Private Soldiers, wishing they were more,
Went to catch a sniper- and then there were four.
Four Private Soldiers discussing M. and V.,
One wolfed the lot which annoyed the other three.
Three Private Soldiers with nothing else to do,
One got promoted, and then there were two.
Two Private Soldiers fighting on and on,
One became a dotard, and then there was one.

One Private Soldier remained in the pink
Till the fifteenth battle of Ypres, I think.
His fate, it appears, was unconscionably sad-
The very last bullet that the Germans had.

Published: Wednesday 4th July 1917
Publication: The Bystander

The Tryst

The mist aboon the burn is stooping,
The mirk has fley'd the winter gloam;
White steeds across the stars are louping.
The moon has girt a flounce o' foam;
My mither waits me at the door,
She kens I've stayed as late before.

To-night I'm try sting wi' my Johnnie,
The laddie wi' the russet pow,
Wi' cunning voice and een sae bonnie,
The soldier's cap aslant his brow.
I aft hae trysted here before:
Why waits my mither at the door
"Frae out the flaught and stow, my lassie,"
He promised yince, "I'll come again,
My fevered drouth will drain the tassie
Of that sweet mou' I've aften ta' en.
I'll bless the day on which I bore
My wifie frae her mither' s door."

Maybe my sicht were bleer frae greeting,
I couldna see his smile sae rare,
Nor feel his lips my reason cheating-
A kiss is best to dree a' care-
Nor heard him whisper as of yore,
"I'll see ye to your mither' s door."

He maun hae led me 'cross the stubble,
Too daft my feet to tread alane;
I thocht about anither's trouble,
I couldna then recall my ain.
It was his mither at our door,
I ken at last he'll come no more."

Written by: Archibald Stodart Walker (1869 – 1934)
Published: Saturday 1st May 1915
Newspapers: The Graphic

To Old Friends Who Fell at The Marne

To Old Friends Who Fell at The Marne
Even as I think of you, dear dead,
You've sped the paths of heroes' ways,
Across the seas your blood made red
The sacred soil of France, to-day.

I brush the tears away; 'tis best
To let the chords of memory
Bring smiles of you who are at rest
After a glorious victory.
Immortal will the praise of you
Linger through all the years to be;
Would I could join with you to-day
The conquering tread of Heavenly feet.

Ah! what a glorious time to die,
Freedom and Honour point the way;
As Britain's hosts in majesty
Break the false power of Hunnish sway.

Even as I think of you, dear dead,
Friends of my youth in school and play,
I envy you the path That led
You glorious up the soldiers' way.

Written by: William C. Jones.
Published: Saturday 26th January 1918
Newspaper: The Graphic

The Welcome

I weep-but in That Other Hall
My little one breaks off her play,
Smiling to hear his dear footfall
Come up the Soldiers' Way.

Once more, swung shoulder-high, she'll ride;
She'll be so proud whisper who's who,
And show him this and that, round-eyed,
The way she used to do.

All-fours-on Death's old nursery, floor-
They romp; through a drear house I roam,
But she, clasping his hand once more,
Will bid him: "Welcome Home!"

Written by: Joyce Cobb.
Published: Saturday 13th January 1917
Publication: The Graphic

Two

Two little golden heads that greet
The coming of the dawn;
Two pairs of little buoyant feet,
That flash across the lawn;
Two little faces innocent,
Lit up by roguish eyes;
Two little voices sweetly blent
When darkness veils the skies.

Two little boys to school must go,
Half smiles and half in tears;
Two eager youths to manhood grow,
Amid the passing years.
Two soldiers, keen to do and dare
Against their country's foes-
Two little wooden crosses where
The battle ebbs and flows

Written by: J. C. Scott.
Published: Saturday 27th January 1917
Publication: The Graphic

The Game

But yesterday we played at soldiers, he and I,
The homeland sun made frolic with his hair,
   As on the daisied lawn he fell to die,
     And just one moment there…
Stiffened himself and held his eager breath.
Toying an instant with Life's bauble, Death.

And now, tho' yesterday is passing young,
   And in my memory a pulsing thing,
I watch the same sweet lawn, my heart is wrung
     By Time's last offering…
Another boy, with shining hair, the same,
Shoulders his little gun and plays the soldier-game.

Written by: Ivan Adair.
Published: Saturday 19th January 1918
Publication: The Graphic

In Memory of an Airman
(Buried by the Germans with every mark of sympathy)

There is a tournament, where knight with knight
Rides forth to clash in lone wide lists of sky,
There over swaying armies in his flight
He rose and fell to die.

And never proud device on coat of mail
Showed gentler knight; he fell with no friend near
To praise; and none to bring the glorious tale
The mourner longs to hear.

But soldiers buried him the soldiers' way;
And fired the last farewell where he must sleep:
"His English mother cries," they said, "to-day
To-morrow ours may weep."

In alien tongue they read beside the grave,
Of other lists beyond the earth and sky,
Where from all lands are mustering the brave,
Who ride with Christ on high.

Written by: Edward Shillito.
Published: Saturday 8th July 1916
Publication: The Graphic
A Young Soldier

Untitled

He dreamed of happy future days,
Of work among his fellow-men,
Of woman's love, of children's ways,
Of pleasures found in book and pen.

Of summer days by ocean's beach,
While glistening sunbeams come and go;
Of snow-capped peaks, he'd strive to reach
Ere from them passed the sunrise glow.

But over all his dreams there falls

The chill grey mist: from out of view
Vanish the radiant, shining walls-
Dream buildings that to him seemed true.

Into the chill, grey mist he goes
With steadfast eyes he sets his gaze
Upon the face of Death, and knows
His power to shatter dreams men raise.

Written by: Elizabeth H. Shillito.
Published: Saturday 30th September 1916
Publication: The Graphic
Our Dead

Untitled

Do you remember, Britain, those who gave you
Youth, health and sight, yes, even precious life,
Clad in the knowledge that the Gift should save you
The scorching breath of strife?
Will you remember, when the fragrant clover
And the red poppies strew the fields afar
With their wild crops, in myriad blossoms, over
Where British ashes are?
Will you remember, when the storm is ended,
And its last echoes find a grave in peace,
All the great glory of that giving splendid,
God's Gift, so like to His?

Written by: Ivan Adair.
Published: Saturday 29th June 1918
Publication: The Graphic

Oblivion

Softly the poppies fall.
Sunsets and dreams and tears,
Brave hopes and barren years-
We leave them, one and all,
Where poppy petals fall.

The rowan's scarlet flame,
The Poet's song-sweet fame,
Old Illion's lofty towers,
The little wayside flowers,
Pan, with the nymphs and fauns,
Bishops and Queens and Pawns-
Still softly over all,
The poppy petals fall.

And Time himself shall lie,
Reft from his majesty,
Beneath that shimmering pall
Where thick and soft and deep
The poppy petals sleep.
While still the poppies fall.

Written by: Agnes-Mary Lawrence
Published: Wednesday 8th November 1922
Publication: The Bystander

The Spectre of Arras

Walk with me softly through the dark city,
Lowering so loftily, scornful of pity;
Shell-torn and shattered, beaten and battered,
Her families scattered-Arras, so cold!

See her poor horses, broken asunder,
Anger it rouses- -list to the thunder!
The Cathedral is shaking, the barricades breaking,
The whole town is quaking-- Arras, so bold!

The Baudimont Gate and the hospice St. Jean
Seem guarded by Fate, for they still linger on,
While the shrapnel is crashing, and drivers are lashing
Mad horses dashing-- -through Arras, the old.

The moonlight is stealing down through the trees,
The- church bells are pealing a message of peace.
The townsfolk returning are joyfully learning
The enemy's turning before Arras of old.

Written by: Lieut, C. G. Reid
Of the London Scottish attached to the Camerons.
Published: Saturday 19th January 1918
Publication: The Graphic

The New Recruits

The Kaiser has declared that, rather than yield, every Dog and Cat in Germany will go to War.

i

I hear the noble Kaiser
Is calling the reserve—
He's calling up the dachshunds
And drilling them to serve.
They make a handsome army,
They can bite and they can pull,
But I ask you what's the matter
With the good old English bull?

ii

I hear the German tabbies
Are going very strong:
The best have all enlisted,
And they're at it all day long.
They've won their stripes already,
But I ask you-what of that?
I ask you-what is finer
Than a strapping English cat?

iii

I know some noble torn cats
Who would gladly volunteer,
And nightly on my back fence
They bivouac this year.
I know, from long experience,
That nothing man can wield
Can still these dauntless animals
Or drive them from the field.

iv

Oh, what a glorious vision
Will our canine army be
With our feline reinforcements!
Not a muzzle shall we see!

We will have the Irish terrier
And the Scottish Aberdeen,
And I'm counting on the poodles
To dress the ranks between.

v

The pug, too, is our ally,
And a very cultured beast,
But inclined to be sedentary
As hailing from the East.
And, while I must admire
His eagerness to serve,
I think, because of asthma,
He'll march in the reserve.

vi

We'll have a Foreign Legion
For the pekinese and pom,
But what I'm really counting
We'll do the fighting on,
Is the Kilkenny brethren,
Who are exceeding firm,
And the heroic Manx cat
Who has no tail to turn.

vii

Oh, dear, kind Kaiser Wilhelm-
As well as pull and bite-
Your pretty little dachshunds
Are very good at flight!
We'll choose a major general
Who, too, can bite and pull-
I mean, a good old war dog,
A fine, staunch English bull!

Written by: Marjorie Patterson
Published: Wednesday 2nd December 1914
Publication: The Tatler

"USQUEQUO, DOMINE?"

We shall shroud his corpse one day,
And lay him upon his bier.
Bound, as by duteous fear,
We shall follow the long lykeway.
And as in his grave we cast
The wreaths we owe to his fame,
Our hearts in our breast will dance—
That now at length we can claim
The rich inheritance
That his living hand held fast.

True! He was our foster-sire-
Through him we were born again,
And raised from the slothful mire
And fed with the tonic of pain!
But in lust he was wild and cruel;
He spared not our Mother's womb.
We have watched her beauty and bloom
Fade, under his reckless rule!

We shall chant his funeral psalm
As we look our last on his face,
In a light that is clear and calm-
A light wherein we can trace
Each line of his features grim.

'Tis in light perpetual
We'll pray, in truth, he may dwell,
So that the memory
Of his strange wild tyranny
May never again grow dim!
Not one of us must forget,
Or nourish a weak regret;
But all with one voice must say:
"He shall lie, where he lies, for aye.
Eternal shall be his rest,
Though it cost a stake through his breast!"

We shall dig his grave one day,
Afar from the sun and moon,
Afar from the trodden way
And the chimings of eve and noon.
In a rapture, grave and divine,
We shall drink of his funeral wine.
And ere the last cup we quaff
We shall call to our wisest and best,
Whose spirit with wit is blest,
To write us his epitaph.

There, on the tombstone white,
We shall read the words they will write,
And thus shall the writing be:
"To War's great memory!
This is the grave of Strife!
Here he lies with his fame,
And all the toll he can claim.
He will prey no more on our life.
The giant hopes that he bred-
They sleep, full quiet, at his head;
The dwarfish fears that he slew-
At his feet sleep quiet, too;
And his sword sleeps, sheathed, in his hand."

A moment more we shall stand,
Held as by lingering ruth,
Scarce believing the truth.
And then, with a cry of glee,
And a long, long sobbing breath,
Out of the place we'll flee-
Back to the work and play
That his biddings no more will stay!
Back to the half-bound sheaf,
And the half-forgotten grief,
And the natural destiny
Of a kind, slow-coming death-
And leave him there to his sleep.

Afar from the sun and moon,
Afar from the eve and noon,
Afar from the fields men reap!

Pray God that it may be soon!

Written by: G. M. Hort
Published: Saturday 14th October 1916
Publication: The Sphere

France's Hymn of Hate

Hate, hate for hate unto that devil-foe,
That forger-king we know.
The corsair's traitor blow;
Hate. O thou God of Hell.
We avenge, by shot, by shell:
We sing of arms, a chant of hate,
The holy canticle of hate!

Let us fling fierce and far our hatred to the sun.
Now we forget all mercy, all pity now have done:
Bury them deep and dark in a mighty winding shroud,
For there's hate beneath our banners, no hate so mad, so proud
Hate, holy word, cry in your thought most deep,
Hate, holy word, cry in your quiet sleep,
Hate, holy word, cry as you awake,
Hate, holy word, cry as your arms you take
Hate, we will teach to every babe thy name;
Each mustard seed, like that of Bible fame,
Shall wax and multiply each fragile head.
Till smothering branches over them shall spread!

We sing of arms, a chant of hate.
The holy canticle of hate!

Too strait for you the earth and sea and skies,
Ferreting out the earth, vile race of spies,
A universal robbery you scheme,
A universe sealed with your seal you dream;
Hate, holy word, forming our reason's might,
Hate, holy word, becomes the right of right.
Hate, holy word, that daily grows in power,
Hate, holy word, our armour in this hour;
Your word can pass current no more than your gold.
You know only actions of baseness untold.

An ambush may lie in each vow that is borne,
And no one will trust you, forever forsworn;

We sing of arms, a chant of hate.
The holy canticle of hate!

In thy pride of a fool, thou thinkest God to cheat.
All-powerful impotent, here now is thy defeat.
Thy chariot has met a hindrance on the way,
And most just justice hath broken thine essay.
Hate, holy word, guides us, a beacon light.
Hate, holy word, shines clear, star of our night.
Hate, holy word, will lead us where we go,
Hate, holy word, will end our savage foe;
Great vessel of the faith, cathedral grave,
Oh! Rheims shall be reborn yea, Rheims again shall shine.
And in a sea of fire this sacred nave,
Which yet shall crown our Kings, shall uncrown thine!

For Alsace Lorraine, the great,
For the human race and State,
Hohenzollern haters,
Tawny traitors,
Hear our war cry madmen. We call
Germans all,
Hate! Hate!

Written by: Jules de Marthold
In reply to Lissauer's German Hymn of Hate, and translated for the New York Times by Miss Barbara Henderson, who made the well-known translation of Lissauer's German War Song.

Published: Saturday 31st July 1915
Publication: The Sphere

Hymn of Hate

French and Russian, they matter not,
A blow for a blow and a shot for a shot!
We love them not, we hate them not,
We hold the Weichsel and Vosges gate.
We have but one and only hate,
We love as one, we hate as one,
We have one foe and one alone.
He is known to you all, he is known to you all,
He crouches behind the dark gray flood,
Full of envy, of rage, of craft, of gall,
Cut off by waves that are thicker than blood.
Come, let us stand at the Judgment Place,
An oath to swear to, face to face,
An oath of bronze no wind can shake,
An oath for our sons and their sons to take.
Come, hear the word, repeat the word,
Throughout the Fatherland make it heard.
We will never forego our hate,
We have all but a single hate,
We love as one, we hate as one,
We have one foe and one alone —
ENGLAND!

In the Captain's Mess, in the banquet hall,
Sat feasting the officers, one and all,
Like a sabre blow, like the swing of a sail,
One seized his glass and held high to hail;
Sharp-snapped like the stroke of a rudder's play,
Spoke three words only: "To the Day!"
Whose glass this fate?
They had all but a single hate.
Who was thus known?
They had one foe and one alone--
ENGLAND!

Take you the folk of the Earth in pay,
With bars of gold your ramparts lay,
Bedeck the ocean with bow on bow,
Ye reckon well, but not well enough now.
French and Russian, they matter not,
A blow for a blow, a shot for a shot,
We fight the battle with bronze and steel,
And the time that is coming Peace will seal.
You we will hate with a lasting hate,
We will never forego our hate,
Hate by water and hate by land,
Hate of the head and hate of the hand,
Hate of the hammer and hate of the crown,
Hate of seventy millions choking down.
We love as one, we hate as one,
We have one foe and one alone--
ENGLAND!

Written by: Ernst Lissauer

The Last Trek
By one of Botha's Army

Steam up! the troopship's waiting, and the last sun gilds the dunes,
The lighters groan and wallow 'neath our squadrons and platoons—
And I'm looking from a taffrail on that God- forgotten shore,
On that shinin' curve of desert where I'll never sweat no more-
All those miles and miles of sand
That our trailing columns spanned,
When we chivvied Franke's rearguard till we struck the hinterland.
We are through with it to-day,
And the boys are good and gay,
For the job is done that brought us swarming down to Walfish Bay.

Looking back, it seems a lifetime -with Mackenzie to the Nek-
Dodging mines with Botha's outfit vanguard on the Windhoek trek-
Pickets on the ridge of evenings Gee the wind was cold at night,
When we left Railhead behind us with the Waterberg in sight.
And the everlasting dirt!
Dust that bit and choked and hurt,
Dust in boots and dust in dixies-dust in swirls inside your shirt.
All that's dead and past to-day,
For we're ducking through the spray,
Heading south for home and mother -fed up full with Walfish Bay.

Far off, too, it seems already! hiking sacks and digging pits-
Watching on a misty morning for those billets- doux from Fritz-
You remember-whistles-scatter! horses snorting, wild of eye,
When that low persistent humming set men staring at the sky And those early rides again
When the sea mist soaked like rain,
And we chased the squarehead outposts to a standstill in the plain-
How it passes like a play
Through my head this time of day,
When the trooper's steaming seaward with her stem to Walfish Bay.

Still, old chum, I'm done with grousing-there were times we've been and had
   Which when we are back in civvies won't seem altogether bad.
  Though we'll relish all the fleshpots we will now and then recall
   Blank's Commando on the war-trail with the high moon over all.
        Knee to knee the sections swing-
        Curb chains rattle-mess-tins ring-
  Two days' rations in the nosebag and we're fit for anything.
        Though the squadrons pass away
        We will think of it some day
When the haze has hid from vision all the sands of Walfish Bay.

  Recollect the heat at Kontas? We were scouting on the flank
When we found that slimy water how the horses drank and drank! Then the
   day we lost the column-plenty buck and loads of wood-
  We were pegged that time, old sportsman but the liver tasted good!
        And the taste of things like these
        Keeps a savour that will please
  Even at a bumper banquet when you sit at home in ease-
        It will seize you with dismay
        That your fancies still can stray
  Back to bully beef and biscuit solid tack at Walfish Bay.

      Written by: Lewis Hastings.
  Published: Saturday 15th January 1916
      Publication: The Graphic

Lines Addressed to the Only Other Captain Left in the B. E. F.

One hesitates to talk like this,
But still-- one must be frank.
Ridiculous tho' it may seem,
The British Army used to teem
With those of humble rank.

Captains, and even Subalterns
Were thick as autumn leaves
And even on the L. of C.
Were heaps of chaps like you and me
With stars upon their sleeves.

A Major was a Major then-
A veteran of war-
A being whose vermilion nose
And massive white mustachios
Inspired a dreadful awe.

Colonels were most impressive things,
And very, very rare:
And when one saw a General pass
One rubbed one's forehead in the grass,
And offered up a prayer.

And no one in his senses dreamed
That any normal man-
However hard he tried to please-
Could be arrayed like one of these,
Unless he toiled and span.

A Golden Age. But nowadays
You hardly ever strike
A home so humble but it boasts
Of having given birth to hosts
Of Majors and the like.

Of every colour, shape and size-
From stern old-fashioned brutes
To bright and beardless boys-one meets
Them everywhere about the streets
Soliciting salutes.

And many grey and warworn men
Are very much depressed
At being targets for the damns
Of Majors in their little prams
And Colonels at the breast.

It seems, however, that unless
Your rank (and pay) are high
You cannot possibly obtain
The fullest value from your brain-
Tho' Heaven alone knows why!

And (as the meanest mind could see
If it was in their boots)-
For Nabobs who are "thinking big"
It must be very infra dig.
To live with Capts. and Lieuts.

But there is nothing here for tears
For one who really thinks!
We two inevitably will
Be used by history to fill
The role of Missing Links.

A Noble Destiny-and so
Why be at all cast down?
Take courage and with me believe
That most uneasy lies the sleeve
That wears a worsted crown.

Written by: Chevron.
Published: Wednesday 12th June 1918
Publication: The Bystander

Winchester

She lies deep-seated in the heart of mothering hills,
A sheltered haven, where no wind that blows
With boisterous ribaldry may disarrange
Her decorous calm and old-world fantasies
Sphinx-like she sits, unmoved, tho' she has seen
The Roman legions, dusty, big with war,
And heard the clang of mailed circumstance
And lordly knights. All these have gone
Into the sunset over yonder hill.
0 citizens of heaven-blest town, rejoice!
For fairer prospect ne'er to men was given
Than that which is thy lot. To view
The sunlight, streaming over Deacon's Hill,
Make subtle patchwork in thy old-time streets,
Or breathe the golden corn to shimmering life
At Giles' foot. No setting could be found
In God's fair earth more happy than thine own,
O wondrous gem of England's wondrous hoard.

Written by: Lieut. L. F. Easterbrook
Published: 8th April 1916
Publication: The Graphic

Untitled

A bleak north-easter chilled the blood;
The driven rain was cold as sleet,
Over the cobblestones the mud
Lay thick along the sordid street;
Under a leaden, lowering sky,
Singing a music-hall refrain,
A Kitchener Brigade went by,
Marching through Merville in the rain.

Young men and strong-and some will die
By bullet, shrapnel, bomb and mine,
Torn by the shreds of steel that fly
From eight-point-two and five-point-nine.
The poison gases' choking breath
Others will feel, and it may be
That some will suffer worse than death,
Starvation in captivity.

I couldn't hear the words they sang,
I didn't recognize the song,
But clear to any listener rang
The meaning, "Now we shan't be long"
At last they heard the sounds of war,
Parades and field-days now were done,
To eager ears the blizzard bore
The grumble of the German gun.

Under a brighter, warmer sky
I fancied I could hear and see
The Roman gladiators cry,
"Salutant morituri te."
The new battalions marched away---
Somehow I' d like to hear again
The simple song they sang that day
Marching through Merville in the rain.

Written by: J. C. F.
Published: 5th January 1918
Publication: The Graphic

Untitled

Whenever I go home again
(If home I ever go)
Will you take up your crutch of pain
(No more for you the bridle rein)
And meet me in the Row?

There, underneath those happy trees,
By shell and shot unscarred
(The lime with its adoring bees,
The poplar surging like the seas,
The plane like spotted pard),

We may assuage the pang that proves
How deep the thrust of war,
And fancy all those thudding hooves
The legion of our lost, which moves
Into our sight once more.

The rat-tail, too, the little bay,
The grey (stained dun) will file
Out of the haze, off hard pave,
To bear our troop of ghosts that day
Who canter up the mile.

Whether I hobble home, or lie
Among these comrades slain,
Death's sting, between a jest and sigh,
No anguish has for those who die
Like theirs who meet again.

Written by: G. M. J.
Published: Saturday 8th July 1916
Publication: The Graphic

The Road to Victory

When the Kaiser, that ungodly man
This very tiresome war began,
Ravaged Belgium, wasted France,
Led us a most unpleasant dance,
Our foe's ambition to impeach
Mr. Asquith made a speech.

Poor Serbia was the next to feel
The brutal victor's iron heel,
She perished under fire and flame.
Hoping for help that never came.
Our good intentions her to teach
Mr. Churchill made a speech.

When Italy saw the dangling prize
Ravished from her tempted eyes,
The tide of battle turned again
From Carso to Venetian Plain.
United counsels to beseech
Mr. Lloyd-George made a speech.

A time came when no margarine
Was on the breakfast table seen;
When housewives though with cash replete
Found it a job to purchase meat.
The need for tightening belts to preach
Lord Rhondda made a splendid speech.

And since it's plain as plain can be
We're on the road to victory.

There's no necessity to explain
The moral of this light refrain.
Only this sacred truth record-
The tongue is mightier than the sword.

Written by: Haldin Davis.
Published: Wednesday 6th February 1918
Publication: The Bystander

Epitaph
(Mother England's Tribute to a Fallen Son)

Trusty, lusty, honest, keen;
In love with life,
And living clean:
Proud of his race; bold, fearless, free:
Such was the man
God gave to me.

Outraged, wrathful, stung to strife;
Loving honour
More than his life:
His Country's call quick answered he:
Nobly he went
To fight for me.

Striving, suff'ring, sorely pressed:
Enduring all,
He gave his best.
A nameless grave across the sea
Now holds the son
War took from me.

Written by: W. Ruffell Rayner.
Published: Saturday 20th May 1916
Publication: The Graphic

Per Mare, Per Terram

"The rules and usages of war were frequently broken, particularly by the using of civilians, including women and children, as a shield for advancing forces exposed to fire." Report of Lord Bryce's Committee on Alleged German Outrages."

"Women and children first!"
That is our way at sea,
Men must endure the worst,
Men of a race that' s free.
When ships go down, our men must drown,
Our men of common clay,
"Women and children first!"
That is the English way.

"Women and children first!"
That is their way on land,
Men of a race accurst,
Men from whom pity's banned.
The world may frown, a woman's gown
Shall shield them in the fray,
"Women and children first!"
That is the German way.

Written by: W K. C.
Published: Saturday 10th July 1915
Publication: The Graphic

The Soul of the Land

There was Peace in the Land;
Men laboured for riches, men laboured for sport,
And some for the joy of achievement alone,
Or the harvest of fame they would reap:
There was pleasure and gain,
Men gloried in riches, men sold and they bought,
And sometimes a Voice spoke of perils unknown-
But the Soul of the Land was asleep.

There was War in the Land;
Men laboured for duty, men laboured for pride,
And some in their passion for free dom and right,
For the Meanings of Life were at stake:
There was anguish and pain,
Men poured forth their life-blood, men suffered and died,
For the glow of the Vision that burst on their sight-
The Soul of the Land was awake.

Written by: Fedden Tindall.
Published: Saturday 25th September 1915
Publication: The Sphere

Home-Coming

Yes, they shall return, each one,
Every lover, every son;
There shall be no empty place
As the armies march apace,
Tho' we recognise them not,
In their garments angel-wrought.

For, with tear-dimmed vision, we
Only see mortality,
Only see the stain of war
Where is laid the hero-star.
In pure linen, white and clean,
They shall pass, our dear unseen,

Down the street they used to know,
With a noiseless step and slow,
Striving, perhaps, our ears to reach
With their newly learn lid speech.
Grief shall close each eye, each ear,
That we see them not, nor hear.

Written by: Ivan Adair.
Published: Saturday 8th February 1919
Publication: The Graphic

Tanks

Poets arise in serried ranks
To hymn the prowess of the Tanks,
And, armed with varied metaphor,
Acclaim these "Wonders of the War"-
"These Living Forts a-belching Flame,"
"These Pachyderms no Hun can tame,"
"These Ichthyosauri of the Battle"
And such like journalistic prattle.
But we, to whom all others yield,
Once more are foremost in the field.
Look at this page and you will see
A Tank, as in reality;
A living T anklet, all complete,
With guns and caterpillar feet,
And steering gear and armoured skin,
And just a fleeting glance within,
Where can be seen, from 1 to 3,
The O.C. Tank enjoying tea.

Written by: Unknown
Published: Saturday 21st July 1917
Publication: The Graphic

Young Soldiers

Only yesterday were they
Chaffing at unwelcome rule,
Measuring study by their play
In the little world of school.

Only yesterday intent
On the limits of their sphere,
Every waking effort bent
On the Now and on the "Here."

Lo! at midnight came the call,
Breaking in upon their sleep,
And their manhood, over all,
Rose to live and run and leap.

Thus, before their day was born,
Many a war-kissed eager lad
Thought of childhood with a scorn
As a thing he never had.

Written by: Ivan Adair.
Published: Saturday 9th June 1917
Publication: The Graphic

Song of a Night Nurse

Anguish and fear and fret
Within this ward so bare.
'Tis midnight yet,
But dawn is in the air.

My eyes with tears are wet,
Fled are the visions fair.
'Tis winter yet,
But spring is in the air.

Sick faces sternly set
Across the low lights stare.
'Tis war-time yet,
But peace is in the air.

Written by: Letty Ison.
Published: Saturday 6th April 1918
Publication: The Graphic

Na Poo
A Typical Topical Tale of the Trenches

Most people have a liking for
Those touching tales about the War
That show the Hero, sword in hand
(Swords are not worn, I understand!)
Leading his men in fierce assault,
And never, never calling "Halt!"
But, just as Victory comes to crown
His gallant effort, stricken down;
Then, later on, nursed back to life
By some sweet duck he makes his wife...

You know the sort of thing I mean?
Well, lately at some pains I've been
(With intervals for food and slumber)
To write one for our Christmas Number,
So here it is. If I were you
I shouldn't bother if it's true
Or false or pretty good, or rotten-
At any rate, it's soon forgotten

Augustus Jones, a. year ago,
Was really quite a Knut, you know,
And in an office drove a pen,
Like scores and scores of other men;
But after office hours were done,
Augustus Jones "was out for fun,"
And spent his jolly evenings with
Miss Emmeline Dorinda Smith,
A charming girl, who found her "boy"
A never-ending source of joy:
To music-halls they loved to go,
Or to some moving-picture show,
And through the darkened streets they'd roam,
Circuitously seeking home.

About the War they didn't care,
Of course, it wasn't their affair;
But all at once, to their dismay,
They found Conscription "come to stay"
And poor 'Augustus (twenty-three,
And timid as a man could be),
Not being among the "Indispensables,"
Found himself in the "Fighting Fencibles"!
But, though the everlasting drill
(He thought) would make him very ill,
Augustus recognised, ere long,
He'd never been so fit and strong.
He gave up cigarettes for pipes,
And actually got his stripes,"
And when the order came "for France"
Got keen as mustard on his chance
Of doing deeds of glittering glory…
-But that is quite another story!

Now for a moment I must wander
From Jones's doings. Let us ponder
On the sad fate of Emmeline,
Who all this sickening time has been
Weeping to think no more she'll see
Her dear Augustus. Victory,
And Glory, such as Victory brings,
Were quite outside her scheme of things:
She only wanted (who can blame her?)
A Husband what could well be tamer?-
But, seeing all the men were gone,
Marriage could not be reckoned on;
So Emmeline, although she might
Have made munitions day and night,
Embarked on something even worse,
And soon became a Red Cross Nurse!

("Oh, help!" I hear you groan, "what rot!
A stale and antiquated plot,
The outcome's plain as plain can be!
Patience, dear reader! "Wait and see!")

To Corporal Jones we now return,
And it will do you good to learn
That our Augustus, truth to tell,
Fought very tolerably well,
And valorously gained-ahem! -
Both the V.C. and D.C.M.,
But also-not so nice a prize-
A nasty cut across the eyes;
A wound of quite a "Cushy" kind,
Which left him, for the present, blind.

And next we see him safe in bed,
A bandage bound about his head,
While at his side, with face so pale,
There sits—No! No! That spoils the tale!
A gentle voice familiar seems
(But wounded men have curious dreams),
Dear fingers soothe his sad contusions
(But wounded men get strange delusions!)

At last arrives the longed-for day
When bandages are laid away,
And sight returns to longing eyes.
Conceive Augustus's surprise,
As from his brow the wrappings fall!...
It wasn't Emmeline at all!!

(There, now! I warned you how 'twould be!
And you're as much annoyed as he:
And really all because I've not
Just followed out the hackneyed plot!)

So Corporal Jones returned to "Blighty,"
But Emmeline, the fair but flighty,
Wedded, the first week she went "out,"
A Major-General with the gout,
Who, though she nursed him very badly
Adored her, passionately, madly…

Moral
A Moral wouldn't come amiss,
I think. But what the Moral is
I've not the least idea! Have you?
Good-bye. Ta-ta. So long. Na poo!

Written by: F. R. Burrow
Published: Monday 27th November 1916
Publication: The Bystander

Gott Mit Uns!

Gott mit uns is their motto engraven
On scutcheon and helmet and sword,
Do the Germans believe in their madness
They mobilised even the Lord?

Gott mit uns as they tear up the treaties
They swore to observe in His name!
As they ravage and decimate Belgium
With cannon and famine and flame!

Gott mit uns as they flout His commandments
In orgies of cruelty and lust
As they torture and slaughter His clergy
And batter His temples to dust!

Gott mit uns as they bid Him to punish
The most hated rival of all!
Is the God of the Kaiser a conscript
And drilled to obey at his call?

Gott mit uns! Is our God not rather
With those they have foully slain?
"For the Lord will not hold him guiltless
Who taketh His name in vain."

Written by: W.K.C
Published: Saturday 21st August 1915
Publication: The Graphic

Highland Lament
The Thin Line at Longuebal

"There has been nothing finer done in the war, or, I believe, in any war, than the way in which the Scotsmen, after four days of unimaginable strain, held and flung back the enormously preponderating numbers of the desperate last German counter-attack. It was what remained of the Highlanders, with a gallant handful of South Africans, who, in a hastily made line, beat back a force of either nine or ten battalions of fresh troops. It is a big thing to say, but there is nothing in all Scotland's fighting history of which Scotsmen have more reason to be proud. By that fortune which helps brave men to do the impossible, they won. Gathering all the men together they could, fragments of battalions, scraps of companies, shreds of platoons they, a mere handful though they were, charged and counter-attacked." The Times, July 25, 1916.

The corn on the Somme was ripe for the reaping,
The scythe of the Reaper, the stalk of the Gael,
O'er the hills of Glenfinnan, the sad stars are weeping,
The winds through the pine trees their coronach wail.
The noonday of Atholl is past to the gloaming,
The heart of Glengarry is black with the mirk;
The lips of Lochaber with anguish are foaming,
And the face of Strathallan is grey as the birk.

The Ogilvie drum is sounding at Airlie,
Clan Chattan's black chanter it pipeth in vain,
For the Chieftains return not they honoured sae fairly,
And the women they moan in the darkness their lane
On the brows of MacDuff the shadows are creeping,
At Cluny the hearthstones yawn empty as wind;
No longer McGregor his vigil is keeping,
And the blue eyes of Appin with tear-mist are blind.

They saw as they fought the Hebrides rising,
A crown in the midst of their unbidden tears;
And a smile out of Morven their wrath was surprising,

And the eddies of Mull whispered low to their fears.
They sprang to the foeman with chanters a-screaming
The pibroch of Donal that's wine to the blood;
They rose and they struck-and then it was seeming
The whole heart of Scotia pour out like a flood.

'Tis the spirits of heroes which watch at the Greening,
And point to the gloaming away to the stars,
And call to the women to hasten their weaning,
And nurture their sons for the greed of the wars;
For this is the destiny, the claymore shall never
Rust in the scabbard, or blunt grow the dirk.
The rune it was written, it speaketh for ever
That the sun of the peace-time must pass to the mirk.

Written by Archibald Stodart Walker (1869 – 1934)
Published: Saturday 26th August 1916
Publication: The Graphic

To the Chestnut Militant

The Village Smithy stood beneath your boughs,
So you should know the sound of ringing hammer;
But otherwise your history allows
Hardly a glimpse of military glamour:
    The trumpet and the drum
Seldom to your secluded precincts come.

Most peaceable of trees! Aptly designed
To grace the landscape or to shade the cattle-
Fitter to play the tree of Rosalind
Than any part in any sort of battle.
    (Though it is true, the Club
Flees from the Chestnut like Beelzebub.)

Not to you, like the Oak, we owe a debt
No Hearts of Chestnut ride upon the billow:
The Pine gives masts; one even finds a wet
And nautical suggestion in the Willow:
    But do you care a jot
Whether Britannia rules the waves-or not?

But now the net of war has roped you in:
The country, in its warlike preparation,
Has need of you; for War we toil and spin;
For War we mobilise the vegetation:
    The portent comes again,
And Birnam Wood marches on Dunsinans.

Whether they shoot you at the foe, or squeeze
A high explosive from your vital sectors;
Whether they pulp you into bread or cheese,
Or make a starch to stiffen the "Objectors"-
    These things I cannot tell:
They are State secrets, dark, inscrutable.

Meanwhile the children think it rather fun,
Infusing play with patriotic ardour,
To gather nuts and range them in the sun,
That they may ripen for the official larder-
Not for our private use,
But with intent to cook the German goose;

A frantic and a foolish bird: perchance
When stuffed with chestnuts, like its friend the Turkey,
It will abate its natural arrogance,
Amend its manners, choose an air less perky
The worst fowl learns a lot
When it sees, on the fire, the imminent Pot.

Written by: R. B.
Published: Saturday 10th November 1917
Publication: The Graphic

A City Sunset
(In War-Time)

Some, when the mystery gathers o'er the housetops
See nothing but a setting swathed in vapour;
Some see the sacred places' swift unveiling,
Holy of holies.

Here where the blues allure to haunts of dreaming,
Where by the park incessant traffic hastens,
All the sweet hush comes strangely stealing earthward, Lapping and lulling.

And in the hush I hear far boom of battles-
In the thick street I see a different concourse
See the worn eyes of tired heroic fighters
Turn to the sunset.

Some see the dust, the blood-stained earth and havoc-
Some see the Grail, and lie there, having seen it.
Some in a flash of spirit see the sunfall
Over far homelands-

See the dear meadows wet with dews of evening,
Long winding roads and homes and village churches,
Or hear this hum of traffic by the parkside
In the great city.

As on an altar for the high uplifting
Flames the same symbol of the eternal presence-
Here with the hearts that ache, the hands that labour-
There with the fighters.

Written by: Arthur L. Salmon.
Published: Saturday 3rd June 1916
Publication: The Graphic

A World of War

May' st Thou, O Lord, with Thine almighty hand
Guide us, Thy fighting men, by sea. and land.
Teach our wild souls to see and understand
Our God is Good.

Far out before, in conflict' s grim array,
Stretch Thou Thy love across the longest day;
Light Thou with it the shadows from our way,
Lord God of Good.

From tangled warp and woof of this vast scene,
Smooth threads of truth into a golden skein,
To work a nobler pattern than has been,
O God of Good.

And may we play the man in all our part;
Yield Thee a real live love of honest heart;
And hold it true, whate'er life may impart,
That God is Good.

When kindly Death shall close our darkling eyes,
In peace unbroken mould these mortal ties,
And sanctify our human sacrifice
By lasting Good.

Written by: David Newton Wemyss.
Published: Saturday 16th March 1918
Publication: The Graphic

Peace and War

I saw him stand where ripening grain
Drank deep the gold of western skies.
There he had made 'mid virgin plain,
A simple free man's paradise.

I saw him next lie broken, dead,
With shell-torn body facing West,
And well I knew his soul had sped
Home to the prairie's peaceful breast.

Written by: Stanley Harrison.
Published: Saturday 16th March 1918
Publication: The Graphic

If Herrick Had Been a Hun

To the War-Lord, Who May Command Him Anything.

Bid me to live, and I will give
My inmost soul to thee;
Or bid me die, and I'll defy
Whatever gods there be.
Bid me the foe to crucify
Upon the nearest tree,
And then to swear an alibi,
I'll do it all, D.V.

Bid me to love, the sucking dove
Could not more harmless be;
Or bid me hate, and I will prate
Of vengeance grim, pardie!
I'll violate and devastate
That isle across the sea,
Though just of late I've switched my hate
To wicked Italy.

Bid me to poison, sack and shoot,
And I will act with glee;
Or bid me burn and rape and loot,
This suits me to a T.
I'm taught to give obedience blind,
And only think through thee,
Thou' st mobilised my very mind,
All-Highest ex-K.G.

In short, I play the super-Hun,
Obeying thy decree;
At times I wonder if I've done
Too much for love of thee.
For just suppose the Allies won,
And dear old Deutschland's overrun,
Thou'lt still have some place in the sun,
But what about poor me?

Written by: W. K. C.
Published: Saturday 12th June 1915
Publication: The Graphic

Ingredients for a Christmas War Story

A panelled hall on Christmas Eve
Where firelight flickers rosily,
A wounded hero home on leave,
A girl for choice a V.A.D.

A meeting in the firelight glow,
Some letters that have gone astray,
A gleaming bunch of mistletoe-
And flavour in the usual way!

Written by: Leslie M. Oyler
Published: Wednesday 25th December 1918
Publication: The Bystander

A War Nightmare
(Brought on by reading the war news and the effusions of the military experts in the Press)

There I stood upon a Bridge-head,
To my right a Point d'appui,
While upon my left a Salient
Stretched for miles in front of me.

All my men were full of Moral,
Elan filled us every one,
We were there to try our best to
Enfilade a German gun.

So I took my trusty Dug-out,
And I filled my Periscope
With the latest High Explosives,
And we started full of hope.

Cutting our Communications
We approached, alas! too soon,
Swathes of Germans waiting for us
In a fortified Platoon.

"Down!" I shouted to O'Leary,
"Duck your head, you silly ass!"
For the Parapet was smothered
In Asphyxiating Gas.

"Who will follow me and Sap them?"
But the 7th Mitrailleuse
Made no answer-for the reason
There was no one to refuse.

I was Decimated badly,
And I felt that all was lost,
But I knew that the Offensive
Must be kept at any cost.

On my right I kept on Sniping,
Which was answered by the Fort
(On my left there was, as usual,
Very little to report.)

Then I sent back to Headquarters
Quite a short but sharp Barbed Wire-
"Am about fed up, am going
To strategic'lly retire."

And just then upon the Plateau
I descried to my relief
Two whole Army Corps, commanded
By Sir John himself-our Chief!

But, alas! on close inspection,
How my heart began to quail,
'Twasn't French; it was Lord Northcliffe
With to-morrow's Daily Mail!

Written by: W. H. B.
Published: Wednesday 4th August 1915
Publication: The Bystander

Two London Boys

"We found two lads of the City of London Regiment sitting in the ditch, frozen and dead. One had his arms around the other, who held fragments of biscuit in the corner of his mouth." A Doctor in Gallipoli.

Their lives went side by side: they ran abreast
To school together played and fought their fights;
Down London streets rang out their merry jest
In noisy London nights.

But school days o'er, they entered side by side
The wild new world till mighty kings made war
And they must die, as wanderers have died,
prom home and London far.

Sealing their early love, abreast they passed
Through the cold night into the unknown sea;
Nor life nor death did part them at the last,
But with them-who is He?

Were those cold, rigid arms, stretched out to save,
Sign of the Arms; that bore the comrades home?
Who was it in the biscuit broken gave
The last viaticum

Written by: Edward Shillito
Published: Saturday 27th May 1916
Publication: The Graphic

Her Renunciation

Sweetheart I thought to stand to you so nearly-
Had we not planned to live and love right nearly-
And see the golden years pass one by one,
In joy and pain, so that we were together-
We minded nothing, just to be together-
Then War was heard-you went to meet the Hun!

The wide world read you died a hero-bravely-
I hold the Cross that shows you acted bravely-
'Tis thickly gemmed with bitter tears of pain!
Yet am I glad to know I shared your giving-
That by no word, no look, I marred your giving,
Since sacrifice can never be in vain!

It is not strange to think of you in Heaven-
You always lived so close to God and Heaven-
And Christ White Comrade- links both you and me,
Until the day He gives us each to other-
Great consummating joy of each to other-
In life and love of ages yet to be!

Written by: Ella E. Walters.
Published: Saturday 12th August 1916
Publication: The Graphic

Made in Britain

DER Kaiser said, "Even I most die.
So ere I to Valhalla fly
I'll seize, meinself and mein ally,
What's made in Britain.

A race of 'slackers' are their sons.
They play their games, we forge our guns,
But soon will rase our blood splashed "Huns"
What's made in Britain.

Their ships I'll sink by treachery,
With mines laid down in neutral sea.
And laugh to th'nk humanity
Was made in Britain.

"And while those mines (with prayer) I sow,
My fleet its courage fierce will show
By sending fishing smacks below-
If made in Britain.

"Their little army! Ach! I laugh.
And then I scatter it like chaff,
And put up for its epitaph,
'Made in Britain.'

"Their power Colonial is a sham.
I'm blood and iron, that's wheat and lamb.
'Twill take its orders from Potsdam
Though made in Brirain.

"The kleine Belgium I'll invade,
Although I once a treaty made.
Who thinks by vows I can be stayed
Is made in Britain.

"I am the War God! And my cup
Of nectar is the belch of Krupp.
To my own shrine I'll offer up
The scalp of Britain."

Der Kaiser thus: He ne'er inferred
The fleet which waited but the word
His ships in Kiel Canal to herd.
Was made in Britain,

Der Kaiser thus: But he forgot
That little army wavers not;
That English, Irish, Welsh, and Scot,
Are made in Britain.

Der Kaiser thus: He could not hear
The tramp of armies closing near
From wide-flung lands which still hold dear
The name of Britain.

Der Kaiser thus: He never thought
Success could be too dearly bought
In Belgian shambles. New he's taught
What's made in Britain.

On horse, afoot, by battery,
The steady hand, the watchful eye,
The will to live, the strength to die,
Are made in Britain.

Uprose, when Justice beat her drum,
The "flannelled fool" a man become,
The "muddied oafs" one blood-red scrum,
All made in Britain.

Slackers till wanted. Up sprang then
From city street, from mountain glen,
An army of a mill on men,
Made in Britain.

When grim Bellona raised her brand,
"Wild women," who had rent the land,
Cried "Truce!" and joined that nursing band
Made in Britain.

When Wilhelm set the world alight,
"Disloyal" Ireland jcined the fight.
For Peace can sunder, War unite
Hearts made in Britain.

When broke the Huns o'er Belgian plain,
"Seditious" India rose amain,
And seven times ten thousand men
She gave to Britain.

When Krupp-cult turned to butchery,
Each "disaffected" colony
Stretched hands to hands across the sea-
Empire of Britain.

The goods they dumped upon our quay
Were lettered "Made in Germany,"
Our troopships' goods were found to be
All made in Britain.

We started in this making way
With Drake-with Marlborough. For they,
Like "little Bobs" and K. of K."
Were made in Britain.

119

Our worship at great Schiller's shrine,
Our love for Goethe's "mighty line,"
For Wagner's harmony divine,
Were made in Britain,

Our hatred of the mine foul-laid,
For curs that Belgium could invade,
For war on infant, wife and maid,
Is made in Britain.

The quest for peace in that dark hour
When Hohenzollern struck for power,
And th' eagle screamed "Devour! Devour!"
Was made by Britain.

Then, God in Heaven! Plunge Thy sword
Through hearts accurst with lust of blood!
And serve us thus, should we, O Lord!
Be false to Britain

Written by: W. J. Moore
Published: Saturday 17th October 1914
Publication: Illustrated Sporting and Dramatic News

Holy Willies Prayer

MY good old Gott, Who in the Heavens dwell,
I fear that things are going none too well,
My big battalions, though they're backed by You,
Have bitten off much more than they can chew,
From Paris, Kales, London, Petrograd,
I'm still as far as ever-- 'tis too bad—
You've let me down a lot since last July,
When I gazetted You as my Ally,
I put it to You frankly-- have You done
Your honest best for my place in the sun?
I'm sore at heart, and think You will agree
It's time I set forth what You owe to me.

I patronised You since I came to power,
And mouthed Your name at least once every hour,
I ranted in my Boanerges vein,
And "Right Divine" was ever my refrain,
I daily lifted up mine eyes to pray
For Your assistance when there dawned The Day,
I made our chosen people take galore
The "Blood and Iron" mixture as before,
For years I sent out spies on every hand,
As Moses sent his to the Promised Land,
I sowed the seed of hate, Your foes to foil,
And fain would reap the fruits of all my toil,
So greatly did I labour in Your service
That lately I have turned a Dancing Dervis,
I study both my Bible and Koran,
And fast through Lent as well as Ramadan.

Since war broke out I've prayed "Thy will be done'."
(Of course with the proviso that we won),
And when with blood of babes my hands were gory,
I murmured piously "Be Thine the glory!"
I've hailed as victories our slightest scratches,
And always mentioned You in my despatches,
I'm sure I've left no stone unturned to please
(Or very few between the Meuse and Lys),
My thousand legions, helped by Krupp's great guns,
Have beaten all the records of the Huns,
Their orders were: Shoot, sack, and then ignite
To make a burning and a shining light,
I've put the Belgian bullies to the sword
And offered on the Altar of the Lord
A holocaust of lives-a million slain-
Burnt off'rings, too, like Termonde and Louvain,
Am I to think that this was all in vain?

Ah, no! You won't desert Your dearest friend,
Who's vowed he'll go on killing to the end,
0 help me, Lord, mine enemies to smite
Both hip and thigh, and show them Might is Right!
Amend the old Mosaic Law, forsooth,
Two eyes for one, a jawbone for a tooth!
Cast out the hireling English Edomites,
Chastise the godless French Amalekites,
And scatter those barbarian Muscovites,
For they're all wicked people who abhor
The cultural advantages of war.
Confound the human race by land and sea,
Compel them all to bow the knee to me,
My claim is eminently fair and just,

I only want the world-- this speck of dust,
"World-power or downfall" is my battle cry,
God of the Hohenzollerns, You've the sky,
Give me the earth, or I shall surely die!

A word of warning- 'ill my folk grow wiser.
They'll always-- win or lose-- trust in their Kaiser,
But if we fail then trouble will ensue,
And Germany will lose all faith in You,
Regretfully I'll have to show who's boss,
And You, of course, will get no Iron Cross.

P.S.-- My style of supplication may seem odd.
But I'm the KAISER-- You are only God!

Written by: Kent Calhoun
OR BURNS BROUGHT UP TO DATE BY BERLIN (A revised version, composed in the light of the Kaisers utterances and the acts of his people)
Published: Wednesday 10th February 1915
Publication: The Bystander

The Rubaiyat of William the Warlord

WAKE! for my banner is at last unfurled
To flaunt its boastful message to the World:
   War to the Death! My Culture to enforce
With Challenge after Ultimatum hurled!

Indeed, indeed, when no one thought of War
   I swore but did I mean it when I swore?-
My little neighbour Belgium to protect,
   Nor let her suffer harm on any score!

Yet, ah! that promise withered like the rose!
   I put my thumb to my Imperial nose
And, tongue in cheek, spread all my fingers out,
   And winked my eye. So now to work-here goes!

Just lately in some tavern, blithe and gay
There gathered Teutons, merry in their way
   With mugs of beer; and one proposed a toast
And bade the others drink; and 'twas "The Day!"

No need to mention what shall be the goal
Towards which my countless legions on shall roll;
   The cursed name stands out in tongues of fire;
It is pre-destined in my heart and soul!

In every boarding house and small hotel
   Already trusty secret agents dwell;
"A valued servant", says each (German) Boss;
   "He's a good waiter, and I know him well!"

There's Fritz-night porter at a club down West-
   Handing his coat to each departing guest,
Yawning the time away till all the lot
   Have one by one crawled sleepily to rest!

See at your elbow everywhere you dine
High-piping Peterkin, with "Wine, sir, Wine!
Hock or Moselle? Sauterne or lager beer?
Until for very shame you can't decline

There is no door but Hans has got a key;
No letter comes that Adolf does not see;
No secret cypher Franz can't understand;
Each he de-codes and posts it on to ME!

The moving lodger writes a choice tit-bit.
Hies to the post, and there gets rid of it;
Some secret news compressed to half a line;
Nor shall you make the meaning out one whit!

All are my spies; and each is bent upon
The noble work that I have sent them on;
Nothing escapes them; so they pry about,
Stopping their month or two, and then are gone!

I give a thousand crosses every day
Of iron, this valiant service to repay,
Till the recipients bend beneath the load.
Murmuring faintly, "Take the things away!"

And that perverted imp I call my son
No end of mischief had already done;
I dare not look to him for help, for he
Is impudently looting-by the ton!

My Zeppelins I lately set a-going
Hither and thither o'er the Ocean blowing,
Filled with my own best gas; but where they are.
Or what on Earth they're up to, there's no knowing!

The worldly hopes I set my heart upon
Have scarcely prospered! I behold anon
My triumph fade like snow before the sun,
And lo my Empire is already gone!

When on an island with a heart of stone
Far from Berlin I wander, all alone;
If any pass through those dim distant Halls
Where once I reigned Turn down an empty Throne

Written by: St. John Hamund
Published: Wednesday 20th January 1915
Publication: The Tatler

To all Fathers and Mothers whose Sons have been Killed in the War

> You plucked him from your heart and sent him out
> To Flanders with a kiss, and tried to smile
> Bravely, and hoped it would be well with him
> (Praying all day and thinking in the night),
> And when the letter came that dreadful day
> You read it through so quietly crept upstairs
> (Like sufferers in a dream who cannot cry),
> Sat on the bed where he was born, half stunned,
> Holding each other's hand-and for a while
> Forgot your other children- did not know
> That One sat with you, living through again
> The Awful Day on which His Son was killed.
> And when they brought Him news that He would die
> (Like you He thought He'd given Him gladly up)
> The Father's heart was broken. All absorbed
> In grief He sat for three dark hours-forgot
> The world and heaven. It was His Only Son.
>
> His greatest gift is yours. He lets you in
> While we, the children, wondering, stand without.
> Come in and know what He still feels and felt,
> You, the Elect, can sympathise with God.
> You know the grief, the love, the awful pride,
> You only know what it means to give the Son.

> Written by: Winifred Ellis.
> Published: Saturday 12th January 1918
> Publication: The Graphic

The Memorial Shrine, Westminster
A Poem on the Proposed War Shrine at Westminster

Here to the Isle of Thorney, where of old
The fishers heard St. Peter's pilgrim cry,
And saw their lowly shrine mysteriously
Lit by the wings of ange's manifold,
Come other angels, who for Beauty bold
Will light a nobler shrine with memory,
Will give Peace homes beneath a happier sky
And drive dull Squalor from her ancient hold.
The dust of those who made our England great
Rests in the hallowed Sanctuary near,
The dust of men who keep her greater lies
In alien graves and under alien skies.
For these a glorious shrine we needs must rear
That with immortal spirits we may male.

Written by: Hardwicke Drummond Rawnsley,
(1851 – 1929) October 31, 1918.
Published: Saturday 26th April 1919
Publication: The Sphere

Untitled

My Ned has gone, he's gone away, he's gone away for good: He's called, he's killed.
Him and his drum lies in the rain, lies in the rain where they was stood.
Where they was stilled,
He was my soldier boy, my Ned.
Between these breasts he'd lay his head.
But now he's killed.

My soldier's gone. His head lies now between two naked stones,
His drum is broke.
There's none to mourn him in the rain, only the rooks which watch his bones:
Which watch and croak.
His great red hand is wasted bare.
That tapped his drum, that touched hair.
Hark ! Not stroke.

But what is this beside my heart, beside my heart that sounds Tap tap, tap tap!
Oh, what is this that beats within, like drummers beating bounds.
Rap upon rap
What, wonder have I felt and heard?
Is it the wing-beats of a bird?
Tap tap, tap tap!

My boy is gone, yet near heart another boy lies now.
Though he be dumb,
He thumps my heart like soldiers thump, he thumps a tow row-row,
To say he's come.
A drummer boy, all gaily dres't.
Will again be at my breast,
Hark ! There's his drum !

Written by: Edwin Smallweed.
Published: Wednesday 29th September 1915
Publication: Kirkintilloch Herald

A Local War Poem
Men of the Knot

The following well-written lines by Mr. C. Hibberd. of Great Haywood—dedicated to the Staffordshire men serving in the Forces—are printed on postcards, which are being sold at 1d., the proceeds being given Mis. Congreve for Red Cross Funds. They are entitled "Men of the Knot—Staffordshire men":

They are mustering far and wide, from the town and countryside.
From the moor and from the river, from the forest and the chase;
They have heard the urgent call and have answer'd- one and all-
For the love of King and country, for the honour of the race. They are real men
—filled with the patriot's fire,
They are real men —men of Mercian shire.
As they proudly march along.
Hearts are high and courage strong.
They out to right a wrong,
Men of the "Knot"- Staffordshire men.

In the days that are to come, midst the busy market's hum.
In the workshop and the factory shall the story oft told.
How in days of direct need Stafford's sons the call did heed.
And did rise to save their country and the freedom that we hold.
Sing we the story—men of the three-fold cord,
Tell of their glory—fighting savage horde,
How they faced the German crew.
Fought as freemen over do,
Fought as Britons staunch and true,
Men of the "Knot" —Staffordshire men.

When their day of duty's done and the victory has been won, And the men
are coming homeward from their work across the sea.
Then we'll greet them with a cheer, with welcome, far and near,
For the men who saved their country, men who kept old England free.
Loudly we'll greet them—gallant and brave and true,
Gladly weII meet them—men who have dared do.
As they homeward march along
Marshailed by a Joyous throng,
Riaise we then the stirring song—
Men of the "Knot"—Staffordshire men.

Written by: Mr C. Hibberd
Published: Saturday 25th December 1915
Publication: Staffordshire Advertiser

The Day
War Poem by a Railway Porter

The following striking poem, -written by Henry Chappell, railway porter at Bath, was published by the "Daily Express," who very properly ascribes the author to the rank of national poet:—

You boasted the Day, and you toasted the Day.
And now the Day has come.
Blasphemer, braggart, and coward all,
Little you reck the numbing ball.
The blasting shell, or the "white arm's" fall.
As they speed poor humans home.

You spied for the Day. you lied for the Day, And woke the Day's red spleen.
Monster, Who asked God's aid Divine.
'Then strewed His seas with the ghastly mins;
all the waters of the Rhine
Can wash thy foul bands clean.

You dreamed for the Day, you schemed for the Day;
Watch how the Day will go.
Slaver of age and youth and prime
(Defenceless slain for never crime)
Thou art steeped in blood as hog in slime.
False friend and cowardly foe.

You have sown for the Day. you have grown for the Day;
Yours is: the harvest red.
Can you hear the groans and the awful cries?
Can you see the heap of slain that lies.
And sightless turned to the flame-split skies
The glassy eyes of the dead?

You have longed for the Day,
you have wronged for the Day
That lit the awful flame.
Tis nothing to you that hill and plain
Yield sheaves of dead men amid the grain;
That widows mourn for their loved ones slain
And mothers curse thy name.

But after the Day there's a price to pay
For the sleepers under the sod.
And He you have mocked for many a ray—
Listen, and hear what He has to say:
"VENGEANCE IS MINE, I WILL REPAY."
What can you say to God?

Written by: Henry Chappell
Published: Friday 28th August 1914
Publication: Western Mail

A Soldier's War Poem

The following verses have been written by a wounded soldier in the Oaklands Auxiliary Military Hospital at Dewsbury

War! War! What is it?
You ask in a mighty way
As if you know all about it.
When you read what your papers say'
A thrill of delight goes through you;
When you read of victory won.
And of the brave deeds of our soldiers,
You utter the words, "Well done!"

While you sit in your cosy parlour
Surrounded by children and wife.
And smile at the glowing picture
That makes you so happy in life.
Just think the khaki-clad ones
Fighting away o'er the foam.
Stopping the barbarous Huns
From reaching your peaceful horn.

War! War! What is it
Of which men crave?
Go ask the heartbroken mother
Whose son found a soldier's grave;
Go ask the grief-stricken widow
Alone in her cheerless home;
Also look at the orphan children
Who are waiting for dad come.

Ye that are happy in England,
Ask not the question again.
But wait for the good time coming
When the Lord Himself shall reign.
Then away with the Jingo spirit.
Let the roar of cannon cease,
And listen —yea, only listen- -
To the Master's voice of Peace.

Written by: Albert E. Ince Sergeant. Worcestershire Regiment Dewsbury, April, 1915.

Published: Wednesday 28th April 1915
Publication: Leeds Mercury

A War Poem

Do the Germans think we're joking in our note they've just received.
Or have they gone clear crazy by the victories they've achieved?
For we told them in that letter things not hard to understand. And it's going respected, whether over sea or land.
When they sank the Lusitania, sent them back a note
That some citizens of this country had gone down with that boat,
And that, if they still persisted in that unfriendly work.
Our duty lay before us. and that duty would not shirk.
They made some good excuses when asked them to explain. And we took it all for granted from such deeds they would refrain.
But they've shown by their actions that their word cannot trust,
But will not insulted, let it cost us what it must.
We have shown them every favour, and are anxious to forgive. But we now see very plainly that in peace we cannot live.
They talk of their concessions, but it seems it's all a sham.
But we want more excuses when they write to Uncle Sam. We're not seeking any trouble, and are anxious to avoid.
But we're going to tell these war lords that we will not be annoyed.
There are ninety million people that our country represents. And they all can be relied on any insult to resent.
We have trusted Mr. Wilson in all that he has done.
And we still can trust his wisdom, for no trouble he will shun. And knows the Yankee nation will stand right at his back.
And. if men and cash can save us, there is nothing he will lack. They had waited for the Arabic, in their cowardly, sulking ship. Caring not for babes or mothers who were taking their last trip.
They took no thought of Yankees when the liner planged to death.
But thanked their Maker they were safe, and still could draw their breath.
Let us pray that Mr. Wilson may be gaided sure and straight. Forgetting not the motto that night is not what's right.
But we cannot sit here heedless when we know our cause is just:
We'll still stand in our motto: In God is all our trust.

Written by: Thomas Hogarth
Published: Friday 19th November 1915
Publication: Whitby Gazette

A War Poem

The world is torn by the battle's roar,
By the crash of the shell—
On the hill—in the dell,
And along by the shore.

But all is in peace in one fair land—
It is free of a foe,
It has little to show,
Of his acts in England.

There flowers bloom and die as of old,
And the birds flit about
And the boys sing and about,
Just the same in England.

Yet the men of this peaceful island
Refuse to dwell there
In that land free and fair;
They dwell not in England.

Though the world is torn by the battle's roar,
They've left peace to crush might,
To struggle for right:
Some have died in that fight,
Far from fair England.

Written by: Rev L. F. E. Foxell
(Curate at St. Andrew's Church, Uxbridge, and Chaplain to the Forces.)

Published: Friday 17th December 1915
Publication: Uxbridge & W. Drayton Gazette

Acknowledgments

With thanks to the British Library for their kind permission to publish the poetry found in this Anthology

www.ingramcontent.com/pod-product-compliance
Lightning Source LLC
Chambersburg PA
CBHW022117040426
42450CB00006B/744